T Are 'σSS!
je
GW00385582

Susie White has gardened all her   ...y-
one years has been creating and   ⌐ᴄ⊓esters Walled
Garden next to Hadrian's Wall ᴉn Northumberland.   Her
organically run garden mixes rare perennials with native wild
flowers in a distinctive, naturalistic style. The garden has
been shown many times on television and has featured in
numerous magazine articles.

Susie lectures widely, designs gardens and contributes to
gardening magazines.   A member of the Garden Writers'
Guild, she has written several books on herbs as well as the
definitive 'Gardens of Northumberland and the Borders'.

CHESTERS
WALLED GARDEN
& NURSERY

Extensive herb and herbaceous
collection in 18th Century
walled garden, National
Thyme and Majoram collections
Roman Herb Garden

The Old Potting
Shed Shop

Sorry no dogs allowed. Please do not
let your children touch the plants as
some are poisonous.

A SENSE OF HERBS

Susie White

Ergo Press
Publishing for Northumberland

A SENSE OF HERBS

Published by
ERGO PRESS
©Susie White 2007
With drawings by the author

All rights reserved. Other than for review or educational purposes, no part of this book may be reproduced, stored in an information retrieval system, or transmitted in any form or by any means, mechanical or electrical, photocopied or recorded, without the express permission of the publisher.

ISBN: 0-9552758-9-X
ISBN: 978-0-9552758-9-0

Printed by Robson Print Ltd, Hexham
Printed using Recycled Paper

ERGO PRESS
5, St Mary's Chare
Hexham
Northumberland
NE46 1NQ
www.ergopress.com

Introduction

I have been growing herbs for a living for twenty two years and in that time I have met and talked to countless visitors at my walled garden by Hadrian's Wall. Some are knowledgeable gardeners or cooks, but the majority of people just want to grow a workable range of herbs that they can cultivate easily and harvest in a relaxed way for the kitchen. The same questions crop up time and again: 'What's the difference between marjoram and oregano?', 'How hard should I prune my rosemary?', 'Which is the best mint for potatoes?' This book is my response to those people who would like a simple, uncomplicated guide to growing and cooking with herbs; something that will give confidence as well as expressing the delight I feel in this wonderful and varied group of plants.

It's not necessary to have a large garden to enjoy growing herbs; the basics can easily be grown in a three metre square. Even tubs by the door or window boxes can be used by those without a garden at all. It is so much more rewarding to harvest plants that you have grown yourself than to buy the forced, less flavourful ones from the supermarket. You also have control about whether or not chemicals are used in their raising. My two-acre garden is run organically and it seems anathema to me to spray pesticides on plants that I am going to eat. Some of the things about cultivation that I have learned over the years I have worked out for myself and are not often found in books. I will be able to share these practical ways of growing herbs in this book.

I made the drawings sitting by the garden door, or in the greenhouse, with a sprig of the real plant lying on my sketchpad. Sometimes a wren would dart near my feet or

a bee would try to land on the specimen I was drawing; the great thing about an organic garden is its great wealth of wildlife. The walled garden faces south, perfectly positioned to capture the sun with lovely, free-draining soil that has been worked for two centuries. It has one of the largest collections of herbs in Britain, the ebullience of the plants given a calm, underlying structure by box hedging and topiary shapes. There are three National Collections, those of thyme, marjoram and burnet (*Thymus*, *Origanum* and *Sanguisorba*) and the many herbs can be culinary, medicinal, aromatic or dye plants. Growing together, they create beautiful borders with their colourful flowers and foliage and their diverse textures and shapes.

At the end of the working day I pick bunches of herbs to take home for the evening meal: tarragon from the greenhouse, parsley from the vegetable beds, thyme from the gravel garden. It has become second nature to add them to the cooking but only because they are there, growing, ready to be picked. The maxim is that if you have something, you are likely to use it. So first of all, I hope this book will inspire you to grow a selection of herbs that are there for you to use and, secondly, that you will feel confident about using them for flavouring. There is nothing more mouth-watering than the smell of potatoes roasting in the oven with lots of rosemary and garlic. And it is so simple to do!

Although I freeze some herbs, and air-dry branches of bay leaves, there are admittedly fewer varieties that can be used in the winter. I don't worry about this, as I like the seasonality of the English garden. There is such a feeling of pleasure in snipping the early chives, smelling the first basil or tasting the summer flowers of borage. Some herbs seem to be perfectly timed for the vegetables that are in season: sweet cicely is at its freshest when the rhubarb is ready to pick. It gives a rhythm to the year, a delight in the changing seasons and if there is less in winter, or I have to use dried herbs, then I am happy with that.

I hope this book will make you feel that herb growing is uncomplicated and that cooking with herbs may be spontaneous and fun. Herbs bring me enormous pleasure as they do to the many visitors to my garden. There can't be another group of plants that are so widely loved and appreciated for the effect they have on all our senses.

Susie White
Chesters Walled Garden
2007

Caution

Herbs can have a powerful effect on the body if taken in medicinal quantities; this can be beneficial, but equally sometimes not, so care must be taken. For example, high or medicinal doses of sage, angelica and fennel should be avoided during pregnancy as they stimulate the uterus. Although I have mentioned in places that there may be contra-indications with some herbs, this does not imply that there are no possible side effects from others.

Please seek advice from a qualified Medical Herbalist rather than attempt self-treatment. The small amounts used in cooking are generally all right. As with anything in life, moderation in all things is a good principle.

Lavenders enjoying a stony, well drained soil

Brilliant orange nasturtium flowers
add colour to a salad

Bees and butterflies love marjoram's
plentiful flowers

Coarse leaves and white flowers
of horseradish in bloom

The sky blue flowers of borage
are a magnet for bees

Rosemary in full flower
in May

Scents of summer:
lavender, roses, chives, golden lemon balm and sage

Thymes come in many different colours

Thymes in full flower in June

Angelica
Angelica archangelica

Like many people, my childhood introduction to angelica was through the bright green candied strips used to decorate cakes. They looked rather artificial and it was a while before I realised that they actually came from the stem of a plant. Now, as a herb gardener and cook, I use angelica quite a lot in spring when its young stems are bursting with flavour. It happily coincides with the rhubarb crop, as does another herb, sweet cicely; adding either to stewing rhubarb means that you can radically cut down on the amount of sugar needed, which is helpful if you need to watch your weight.

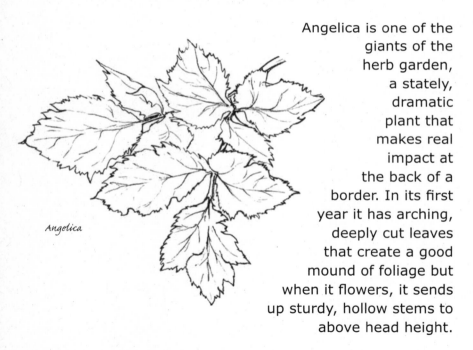

Angelica

Angelica is one of the giants of the herb garden, a stately, dramatic plant that makes real impact at the back of a border. In its first year it has arching, deeply cut leaves that create a good mound of foliage but when it flowers, it sends up sturdy, hollow stems to above head height.

These are topped by green globes of flowers that later produce copious amounts of seeds.

Angelica is neither a perennial nor a biennial but is monocarpic. This means that it dies after flowering, so it is possible to delay its end by stopping it from completing its life cycle; in other words by cutting out any flowering stems that emerge. Since, however, it seeds itself so freely, it is easy, after a couple of years of getting it established in a spot, always to have plants on the go, ready for picking. Don't forget, though, to cut off most of the seedheads before they drop or you will have a forest of angelica! Angelica is such a fine plant that it is often included in a flower border. The purple leaved *Angelica gigas* is even more decorative, combining especially well with silver leaved plants.

Candying the stems is not a quick process and involves boiling them, steeping them in sugar, resting this for a few days, boiling and sugaring again and finally drying in the oven! Only the young stems can be used or they are too tough, so they need to be picked in April or May. I find it easier to buy candied angelica from my local delicatessen and to use the leaves instead for sweetening fruit. To reduce the tartness of sharp plums, apples or rhubarb, I add a couple of its large, complete leaves and gently stew them. They also go well with jams and preserves as does the root, which can also be used to add flavour. The leaves can be chopped and used to flavour salads or fish dishes. I love the smell of angelica. When I have had to dig up a plant, probably because it was in the wrong place, I can't resist tasting the hollow stems and inhaling the strong, perfumed smell of the roots.

Angelica
Plant type: Monocarpic
Height: up to 2.5m
Ideal conditions: Deep, damp soil, shade or sun
Uses: Culinary, medicinal, fixative for pot pourri

Basil
Ocimum basilicum

Basil is now one of the most popular and widely used herbs, thanks to the surge of interest in the Mediterranean diet. Supermarkets stock fresh basil all year round and pesto is ubiquitous, used in ready meals, dips and biscuits everywhere. Although it is not the easiest herb to grow at home, the flavour is so wonderful, evocative, as well as stronger than the shop-bought herb, that it is worth the effort. Germination is not difficult but the key to successful growing is not to sow too early. Basil easily rots off at seedling stage without the warmth of the sun to bring it on. It then needs maximum light and careful watering; a small amount of water each morning in a tray under the pot that the plant must absorb within a couple of hours. Don't ever leave it standing in water for longer as it hates having wet feet! And remember to pinch out the tips to prevent it flowering.

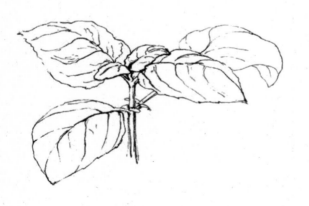

Basil

I grow lots of basil in pots, some alternating with the tomato plants in the greenhouse as companion planting to deter insect pests. This happy relationship continues into the kitchen where basil and tomatoes seem made for each other.

My husband makes wonderful pizzas using local flour and a simple, home-made tomato sauce: blended, softly cooked onions, garlic, virgin olive oil, tinned Italian plum tomatoes, all slowly reduced and thickened with the late addition of plenty of basil leaves. More fresh basil is added to the pizza but tucked under the mozzarella cheese so that it doesn't go crisp and dry.

To keep its fresh taste, basil should be eaten raw in salads, as a garnish or included just at the end of cooking. The leaves shouldn't be bruised, so I like to cut it up with scissors or leave them whole. They are bruised, however, when it is pounded in a pestle and mortar to make pesto sauce, together with pine nuts, garlic, Parmesan and olive oil. Basil seems the epitome of summer, conjuring up images of eating outside, its leaves sprinkled on colourful aubergines, peppers, courgettes and beans.

There are many varieties of basil that can be grown from seed. Some have attractive purple leaves such as 'Dark Opal' or 'Purple Ruffles' or have an extra flavour of lime, liquorice, lemon or even cinnamon. Greek or Bush basil makes a lovely compact plant especially for growing on windowsills or in pots by the kitchen door. Holy basil is the kind grown in Hindu temples and used in Ayurvedic medicine. It has a strong, spicy scent and is highly revered in India and Thailand.

Basil
Plant type: Annual or short-lived perennial
Height: up to 40cm
Ideal conditions: Full sun, min temp of 10º C
Uses: Culinary, medicinal, insect repellant

Bay
Laurus nobilis

An ancient herb with a rich history, bay is an aromatic shrub with leathery, oval leaves that are much used in cooking worldwide. The symbolic 'laurel wreath' denoting success was made of edible bay leaves and should not be confused with the poisonous leaves of common laurel (*Prunus laurocerasus*). The importance of bay as a victory crown is reflected in some prestigious words: Poet laureate, baccalaureate and bachelor (of Arts). When worn on the head it was even believed to protect against all manner of ills, including being struck by lightning!

Bay can become a large shrub in a protected garden but most often it is grown in a pot that can be put somewhere cool but frost-free in winter.

Bay

I grow it in the soil of an unheated greenhouse and have to cut it back regularly to stop it growing through the roof; yet I have had bay killed by winter just on the other side of the glass. Because it tolerates clipping it is often used for topiary. I also grow a golden variety of bay and one with narrow, willow-like leaves.

Mostly pest free, they can however get attacked by scale insects; these limpit-like pests can be controlled by scrubbing them off with a soft toothbrush or with a biological control (a natural predator).

Bay leaves can be used fresh but I find the flavour can be a little bitter and that a better one develops when they are dried. I air-dry a whole branch and leave it in a dark kitchen cupboard to pick off leaves when needed or store them in a dark jar. An ingredient of the classic *bouquet garni,* they add a richness and depth to soups and casseroles, stockpots, stuffings, marinades, meat and fish dishes. Its flavour infiltrates a homemade tomato sauce and makes a subtle difference to salmon cooked in a foil packet in the oven. A leaf or two is good with basmati rice or put whole into a curry, to be picked out before serving. Bay is equally good in puddings and is used to scent custards and milk for desserts.

To make a bouquet garni
This is a small bunch of herbs held together with string and used to flavour soups, stews and stocks during cooking. Take a bay leaf, a few sprigs of parsley and a few of thyme, wrap them in a leek leaf or bunch together with a piece of celery. Take out before serving!

Bay
Plant type: Large shrub, small tree or as a pot grown specimen
Height: usually up to 12ft in Britain
Ideal conditions: Sun, well-drained soil and a sheltered microclimate
Uses: Culinary, medicinal, aromatic

Borage
Borago officinalis

Borage is a true summer herb, conjuring up images of blue-sky days, foraging bumble bees and eating outside. Its euphoric reputation goes back many centuries, from the days when Pliny described it as making 'men joyful' to Gerard writing in his Herbal that it 'drive away all sadnesse'. There is something about this cottage garden herb that does indeed lift the spirits; perhaps it is the star shaped azure flowers echoing the sky or the fresh and vital cucumber scent of its leaves.

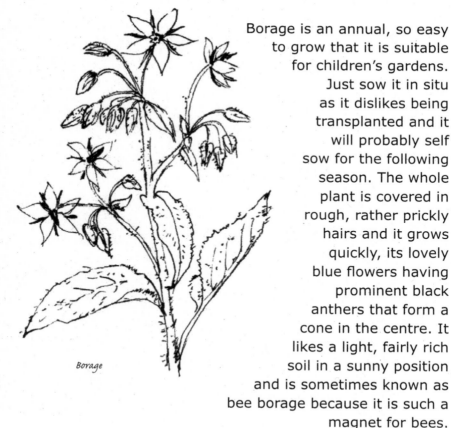

Borage

Borage is an annual, so easy to grow that it is suitable for children's gardens. Just sow it in situ as it dislikes being transplanted and it will probably self sow for the following season. The whole plant is covered in rough, rather prickly hairs and it grows quickly, its lovely blue flowers having prominent black anthers that form a cone in the centre. It likes a light, fairly rich soil in a sunny position and is sometimes known as bee borage because it is such a magnet for bees.

The most famous use for borage is for garnishing Pimms No1, the gin-based drink mixed with lemonade, fruit, mint and ice. Served at Wimbledon, rowing regattas or cricket matches, it seems a quintessentially English summer drink, redolent of picnics or an afternoon spent outside the pub. Too often it is served with a wedge of cucumber or just mint, instead of the unique and refreshing taste of borage.

The flowers can be frozen in ice-cubes and used to decorate drinks or crystallised for cake decoration. I like to use borage in salads, combining its wonderful blue with the orange of marigold (calendula) petals or the brilliance of nasturtiums. If you hold the back of the flower head with one hand and gently tease off the star-shaped ring of petals with the other, you can detach the flower without its black anthers. The young and most tender leaves add a juicy freshness to salads and cheese or cucumber sandwiches.

As well as the usual blue flowered borage, there is also a pure white form which is rather beautiful. I also grow a perennial borage, *Borago laxiflora,* which has drooping flower heads shaped like little pixie hats. I remember overhearing a couple of women in my nursery tut-tutting and saying that borage was an annual and it must be labelled wrongly!

This herb is now used as a commercial source of gamma-linolenic acid. The concentration in its seeds is approximately twice the level of that in Evening Primrose Oil and has been shown to be beneficial for a wide range of conditions. Perhaps there really is something in the idea that borage raises the spirits!

Borage
Plant type: Hardy annual
Height: 2-4ft depending on soil
Ideal conditions: Sun, light soil but not fussy
Uses: Culinary, medicinal, bee plant

Chamomile
Chamaemelum nobile

Chamomile is the plant that was famously given to Peter Rabbit, one tablespoon before bedtime, after his escapade with Mr McGregor. It is a sedative herb that acts mainly on the digestion and just the thing for a rabbit that has slipped under the gate and overeaten on illicit produce! It is the white daisy flowers that are harvested and dried to make chamomile tea bags. One of the most popular herb teas, its mild sedative qualities make it ideal to drink in the evening if you suffer from insomnia, stress or anxiety. And once the tea bags have cooled, you can put them on your closed eyes to relieve tiredness.

This is a heady, scented herb that has been used for over two thousand years. The Greek name for it meant 'earth apple' because of its smell and the Spanish word for chamomile is *'manzanilla'* meaning 'little apple'. The evocative apple scent that is released from its ferny foliage led to it being grown, especially in Tudor times, in the form of raised chamomile seats and lawns. Sir Francis Drake played his famous game of bowls on a chamomile lawn before the arrival of the Spanish Armada. On such a large scale, the scent must have been truly wonderful.

To make a chamomile lawn, choose a sunny, well-drained spot that has been well prepared: finely levelled, all stones removed and lightened with some sand and seaweed fertiliser worked in to it. The best variety to plant is called 'Treneague'. This does not flower and grows in a beautifully compact way, so if you want to harvest the flowers for tea you will need to plant the original species in a separate bed. Young plants should be spaced a hand's width apart and kept well weeded until they knit together to form the lawn. It will take light walking on or sitting on but not heavy use; the best way to a really sensual experience is to walk on it barefoot! For a much smaller 'lawn' you can plant up an area between flagstones especially in a place where you like to sit outside.

Non-flowering chamomile has to be produced from rooted offsets but one plant will give a dozen of these in a season. Flowering chamomile is easy to grow from seed but the lovely double form will also need to be grown from cuttings. This was developed by medieval herbalists to increase the usable size of the flower heads for medicine and it is a very pretty cottage garden plant. Its shaggy pompom daisies have pale yellow centres and it flops over the edge of a path, giving a sweet apple smell whenever you brush against it.

chamomile

Chamomile may cause a reaction in people who have allergies, especially towards members of the daisy family.

Chamomile
Plant type: Evergreen perennial
Height: Flowering chamomile 25cm, 'Treneague' 8cm
Ideal conditions: Sunny, open position, well drained soil
Uses: Aromatic, medicinal, pot pourri, herb tea

Chervil
Anthriscus cerefolium

It is a pity that chervil is not as widely grown here as it is in France since it has a very pretty lacy leaf and a delicate flavour. It is also surprisingly winter hardy and young seedlings that germinate in early autumn can make really usable plants the following year before some of the other herbs are big enough to cut. It can even be grown in damp shade, a position that many herbs will not tolerate. The tiny white flowers are followed by a profusion of thin, black, spiky seeds, so if you leave a couple of plants to self seed there will be plenty for the next batch.

Chervil is very easy to grow and successional sowings at two-week intervals just take minutes to do. It grows very well in containers, being quite a neat, small herb. If planted in full sun it may bolt and although it turns a beautiful reddish purple colour as it goes over, it is the young leaves that are needed for cooking.

These leaves are a really bright green, finely divided and decorative, so you can imagine that they look good on a white plate. I think it makes an even more attractive garnish than parsley; it is just a bit more unusual and eating it raw means that its fleeting anise-like flavour isn't lost through cooking. In France, you sometimes find bowls of finely chopped chervil are served alongside soups and sauces for you to add your own. The flavour is lost in drying but, surprisingly, it will keep well in a sealed container in the fridge.

If you do cook with chervil, add the chopped leaves at the very last minute and err on the generous side. Because of the delicacy of its flavour, this is a herb that goes best with foods that do not taste too strong in themselves: potatoes, rice, eggs, salads, steamed or poached fish, chicken, creamy soups, herb butter and mild cheeses.

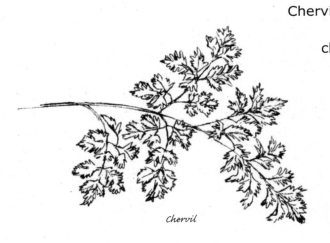

Chervil

Chervil is one of the four ingredients of the classic *fines herbes,* along with parsley, chives and French tarragon. This is added to omelettes and other egg dishes as well as giving the flavour to a Bernaise sauce.

As with other herbs, it is good to experiment. I think it is delicious with a bowl of mussels cooked simply in white wine and a little garlic, or baked with salmon or trout in a foil packet with butter, white wine and a few chives. Its freshness and lightness make it ideal for spring vegetables: carrots, young asparagus, new potatoes, the most tender peas and beans and young leaf salads.

Chervil
Plant type: Hardy annual
Height: Up to 60cm
Ideal conditions: Damp shade, versatile
Uses: Culinary

Chives
Allium sativum

It couldn't be easier to grow chives, which may be why they find a place in so many people's gardens. They make dense clusters of bulbs that are able to be split, pulled apart, replanted, generally treated carelessly and still come up! I have several rows of chives in my vegetable garden so that they can be cut down in rotation throughout the growing season; by cutting a clump back to ground level, you force lots of young, fresh leaves for cooking. This can be done three or four times, each time producing tender leaves.

Chive flowers are really beautiful – miniature versions of the trendy alliums to which they are related. Their purple globes are made up of numerous bell-shaped flowers with a strong onion taste. You can use a whole flower head to decorate a salad or break up the individual florets and toss them amongst salad leaves. I leave some clumps of chives to flower so I can use them in this way (and attract bumble bees) but cut the rest back to prevent the tough, hollow flowering stems from getting mixed up with the chopped leaves.

You can use chives whenever you want a mild onion flavour. I hold a big bunch and just cut them up with scissors into small pieces, adding them at the end of cooking, or raw so as not to destroy their flavour. They are delicious with eggs, cold and hot soups, creamy cheeses, potato salad, sauces, and are one of the ingredients

Chives

of *fines herbes.* Chives make a healthy garnish for steamed vegetables and can be baked into biscuits and cheese scones. A delicious simple starter is made from scooping the seeds from juicy large tomatoes and stuffing them with creamy goats cheese, virgin olive oil, fresh pepper and chopped chives.

Chives grow quite happily in containers so you can always find somewhere to put them and avoid buying the ones in expensive plastic packets that have clocked up many food miles and been grown with chemicals. The closer you have them to the house, the more likely you are to think, 'Oh, I'll just nip out and get some chives'.

There are several very decorative types of chives that look good in the garden as well as on the plate. Varieties such as 'Forescate' (large bright pink heads), 'Black Isle Blush' (pink with rich pink veining) and 'Pink Perfection' (a deep pink) look wonderfully ornamental in a flower border. Garlic chives have flat leaves and a starry white flower head. They are grown extensively in China where they are blanched under pots to re-sprout in the dark as tender white or pale yellow leaves. They have a mild garlic flavour and the flowers look pretty in salads.

Chives
Plant type: Clump forming perennial made up of bulbs
Height: 30cm
Ideal conditions: Rich, moist soil in sun but versatile
Uses: Culinary

Coriander
Coriandrum sativum

Anyone who likes Indian or Thai food will be familiar with the taste of coriander. In seed form it is considered a spice, when fresh as a herb (also called cilantro in America). The smell of its leaves is quite unique; it has a distinctive, biting, citrusy taste that you either love or hate. Personally, I love its delicate, lacy foliage and extraordinary flavour and find its pungency is just what is needed to compliment the richness of spicy food. It is very attractive in leaf form, like a more rounded and finer version of parsley, so its use as a garnish makes the most of its pretty shape.

Coriander

Coriander is another of those herbs best added at the end of cooking. Its flavour is robust enough to work with green chillies and garlic in fresh chutneys, curry pastes, spiced soups, chicken, pork and fish. You can toss it into stir-fries or use it to pep up a rice salad. It adds extra zest to a salad dressing or in a Greek side dish of creamy yoghurt, olive oil, fresh coriander and mint.

And for something special, you can foil-roast monkfish with chilli, lemon grass, lime, garlic, ginger, coriander and coconut milk. It has a natural affinity with all of these exciting oriental ingredients.

To have a regular supply of coriander leaves for cooking it is a good idea to sow it in rows at three or four week intervals.

A hot summer tends to make this herb bolt and produce seed, the leaves then becoming useless for harvesting (though you can dry the seeds and use them in curries). The flowering plant looks pretty with its delicate white flowers and spherical seeds; these have a rather unpleasant scent when green but mature to give a warm, tangy citrus-like taste. A now classic combination is to use crushed coriander seeds in carrot soup but they are delicious with sweet things as well: apple pies and cakes, pine nut torte and fruit loaves.

If you need to buy fresh coriander you will usually find far more generous, loose bunches for sale in oriental supermarkets than those ready packaged in plastic boxes – and at a better price. I have also had good success with sowing dried coriander seeds from the large, cheap packets on the spice shelf of Chinese shops. Although a variety grown more for seed, it is so cheap compared to garden centre packets that you can keep sowing it liberally. It helps to crack the seeds gently with a rolling pin and soak them overnight to get better germination. You can then have plenty of this pungent, fragrant herb for cooking all summer long.

Coriander
Plant type: Hardy annual
Height: 60cm
Ideal conditions: Well drained soil in sun, but kept moist with a mulch
Uses: Culinary, medicinal

Dill
Anethum graveolens

Fennel and dill look quite similar but are quite different plants: dill is an annual, fennel a perennial, dill has a blue-green colour whilst fennel is bright green. They both have beautifully delicate ferny foliage and quite similar uses in the kitchen, but whilst fennel tastes of aniseed, dill has a crisp sweet flavour like a mixture of anise and caraway. It is a very pretty herb that looks attractive as a garnish. Its leaves are so fine that they look like threads and, as it matures, it is covered in tiny yellow flowers followed by flat seeds.

Dill is easy to grow in the garden, best sown in situ in rows at three-week intervals for a season of plenty. In a dry summer it will bolt so keep an eye on the watering or it will run to seed. Some varieties have been bred for leaf production such as 'Dukat', 'Hera' or 'Fernleaf' and are less likely to bolt. Both leaves and seeds are used in recipes so it is good to have plants ready at different stages to produce both. The leaves are sometimes referred to as 'dill weed'.

To start with dill leaves, the most famous combination is of dill and salmon as in the Scandinavian gravlax: raw salmon that is marinated in masses of this delicious herb. Dill is a favourite in Sweden where it is cooked with crayfish or potatoes, used to flavour the white sauce served with meatballs or a pungent mustard dill sauce for fish. Crushed dill seeds give a tangy flavour to homemade cheese biscuits. I like to snip dill leaves over summer salads, cucumber soup, boiled new potatoes or thick and creamy Greek yoghurt. You can make a simple herb mayonnaise by adding dill, lemon juice and seasoning for serving with fresh crab, to be eaten in the garden with a glass of white wine!

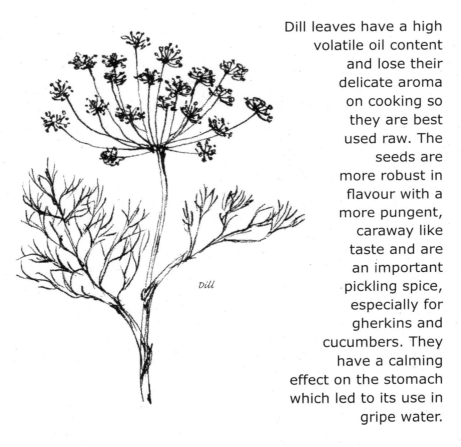
Dill

Dill leaves have a high volatile oil content and lose their delicate aroma on cooking so they are best used raw. The seeds are more robust in flavour with a more pungent, caraway like taste and are an important pickling spice, especially for gherkins and cucumbers. They have a calming effect on the stomach which led to its use in gripe water.

In fact its name comes from the Norse 'dilla' which means to lull, because it was used to lull babies to sleep. I think the name 'dilla' is a much prettier name for this appealing herb.

Dill
Plant type: Hardy annual
Height: 60-80cm tall
Ideal conditions: Well drained soil in sun,
but with adequate watering
Uses: Culinary, medicinal

Edible Flowers

Many of the herbs in this book have colourful flowers that look visually stunning when decorating food. A leafy summer salad can be a vibrant kaleidoscope of orange, blue, purple and red from marigold, borage, chives and nasturtium. Their seasonality makes them more precious; instead of having them all the time, we can look forward to flowers that mark the rhythm of the year. The white stars of wild garlic are a celebration of spring, the purple of lavender symbolises summer.

The flowers have a mild taste of the herb itself, so rosemary, thyme, marjoram and hyssop echo the Mediterranean flavours of their leaves. Their colours are sumptuous; hyssop is a deep blue, bergamot a fiery red, coriander and chervil lacy white and mint a sparkle of mauve florets.

There are other flowers in the garden that can be eaten but that are not generally used in cooking. The delicate pale petals of the primrose and the richer yellow of the cowslip, though used in wine making and herbal medicine, are not immediately thought of as salad ingredients. Rose petals which form part of Middle Eastern cooking, come in a great variety of colours from the subtle shades of the wild rose to the rich deep pink of *Rosa gallica* var. *officinalis*, the Apothecary's Rose. The little blue and yellow 'faces' of the heartsease pansy, the pinkish tubes of the honeysuckle, the pink of mallow and royal blue of cornflower, all add different textures and colours to food.

Nasturtium flowers have a hot and spicy flavour to accompany their exotic, dazzling colours. They can now be bought in some supermarkets for adding to salads or stuffing with feta cheese, chopped walnuts and a little basil as an unusual starter. A favourite with children because they are so easy to grow, their peppery leaves add a mustard like bite to sandwiches and their buds can be pickled in vinegar rather like capers.

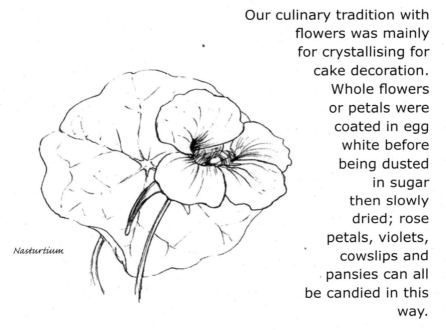
Nasturtium

Our culinary tradition with flowers was mainly for crystallising for cake decoration. Whole flowers or petals were coated in egg white before being dusted in sugar then slowly dried; rose petals, violets, cowslips and pansies can all be candied in this way.

In oriental cooking there is often great care taken in presentation; in Japan, vegetables are often sculpted to look like flowers, whilst the petals of the annual chrysanthemum, *Chrysanthemum coronarium,* are sold fresh or dried for eating in salads or stir fries. Jasmine flowers give a delicate perfume to tea. There are, however, many garden flowers which are poisonous, delphinium, aquilegia, lily-of-the-valley, lupin, foxglove and monkshood to name but a few, so only eat those that you definitely know to be edible.

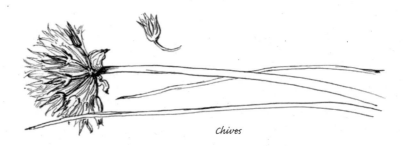
Chives

Fennel
Foeniculum vulgare

I feel that no herb garden should be without delicious, feathery fennel but you may be put off planting it because it can reach 2m in height. Although it does look stunning when allowed to grow to its natural span, fennel can be cut down two or three times during the growing season to keep it much shorter – and provide a continuous supply of young, fresh tops for cooking. This fennel is not the same as the vegetable that is also known as Florence fennel and which has swollen white bulbs. They are dug up when ready to harvest whereas fennel, the herb, is a perennial plant.

With its sweet aniseed flavour and vibrant, green thread-like leaves fennel is a beautiful plant. If you do let it flower, its golden flat tops attract bees and other beneficial insects to the garden. It is a good idea, however, to cut it right down to ground level before the seeds form, otherwise it will self sow with abandon. I learnt this the hard way years ago when I could clearly see in spring the route I had taken to the bonfire the previous autumn from the thick line of fennel seedlings!

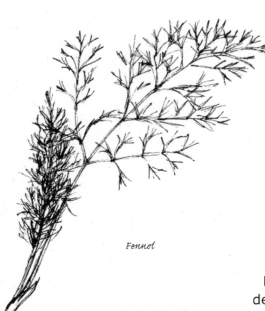

Fennel

Like dill, fennel is delicious with fish; I like

to stuff the cavity of trout or sea bass with loads of fennel plus a little marjoram and chives and bake it or cook it on a barbecue. In southern France, fish is cooked over charcoal between two thick mats of fennel which part steam it, keep it moist and give it a subtle flavour. As a salad ingredient, fennel is at its best when young and tender, so forcing re-growth by cutting it down is very practical. The chopped leaves really enhance a fish pie and are tasty in a dressing for whole fish, large prawns or lobster.

Fennel's popularity in cooking is not just because of its taste; it has a double use as it also aids the digestion of oils and fats. The seeds have a warm, aromatic and sweet taste and can be bought in tea bags for a digestive drink after meals. Chewing the seeds is supposed to take the edge off your appetite, which may be useful in slimming! In medieval days, people would smuggle them into church and chew them to hold back their hunger during long sermons.

There is a very beautiful bronze form of fennel (*Foeniculum vulgare* 'Purpureum') which is often used at the back of herbaceous borders where its tracery of purplish foliage provides a good foil for other plants. It can be eaten in just the same way as ordinary fennel, in fact its young, silky, chestnut-coloured tops look even better as a garnish.

Fennel
Plant type: Perennial, sometimes short lived, but self seeding
Height: 2m
Ideal conditions: Sun, light soil
Uses: Culinary, medicinal
Comments: Avoid overuse during pregnancy

Garlic and Wild Garlic
Allium stativum & *Allium ursinum*

Despite its association with the Mediterranean, it is perfectly possible to grow garlic in Britain. It needs a light soil, so growing it on well-drained deep beds is a good idea. You can plant cloves bought for cooking, but in order to get the right variety for your area, it is better to buy garlic for planting in the same way as onion sets. There are some 450 varieties worldwide and the supermarket garlic may not be suitable. One particular strain has been developed by the Really Garlicky Company in Scotland; this has large cloves, is easy to peel, and is truly delicious. The fact that it is field grown near Inverness shows it can be successful in our climate.

Garlic bulbs split into cloves and these can be planted individually at 15cm apart and 2.5cm deep. In very light soils this can be done in autumn, for colder or heavier soils in spring, and can be set out in rows in the vegetable garden. Apart from the satisfaction of producing your own, it is then possible to grow it organically. I am never without garlic in the kitchen as it is used in so many different dishes as well as having well documented health benefits; it is said to lower blood pressure and cholesterol, prevent heart disease and colds, and to have antiseptic and anti-bacterial juice. No wonder the builders of the Pyramids were in part paid in garlic to keep them fit and healthy.

It is when garlic is cut or crushed that its strong scent is released. It is essential in so many recipes: garlic butter and bread, pasta dishes, with meat, fish and seafood, Mediterranean stews, salad dressings, mushrooms and the heady garlic mayonnaise *aïoli*. But if you find its taste too strong, try roasting whole bulbs with a little olive oil in a foil packet for an hour and a half. This long, slow cooking results in succulent garlic that has a sweet, nutty flavour and is delicious simply spread onto toast.

One of the glories of spring is the sight and smell of wild garlic luxuriating in vast drifts in our woodlands. Every part of this plant can be used: its beautiful white starry flowers, its luscious wide green leaves and its pale elongated bulbs. I find the leaves are the most useful and can be easily chopped or cut with scissors for putting in soups, stews, rice dishes, salads, omelettes or curries. The flavour is mild, especially when cooked, and for me it one of those seasonal foods that I look forward to each year.

garlic

Garlic
Plant type: Bulb made up of up to 15 cloves
Height: Leaves grow up to 60cm
Ideal conditions: Sun, light soil
Uses: Culinary, medicinal

Wild Garlic or Ransomes
Plant type: Bulb
Height: 40cm
Ideal conditions: Woodland plant that can also grow in part sun but can be invasive in gardens!
Uses: Culinary

Herbs in the wildlife garden

Herbs are sensual plants, filling the air with scent, delighting us with their flowers and bringing taste and colour to cooking. As well as all these wonderful attributes, they have another side: that of attracting wildlife into the garden. I run the walled garden organically and this is tremendously important to me. It is not just about finding alternatives to chemicals (though this is part of growing for food and medicine) but also about a whole attitude of mind that sees the garden as a unity. Over the years it has achieved a balance that has made the use of chemicals redundant, but this is aided by the abundant bird life, benevolent insects and other wild creatures. They are attracted by the gardens fullness, its bountiful nest sites, food sources and ponds. There is constant movement from birds, bees and butterflies and herbs are a vital part of this.

Many British wild plants have been tamed over the years, brought into gardens where they could benefit from improved soil. Native insects, such as wild bees, cannot always get nectar from highly bred, double flowers and they really benefit from having simple, species plants in our gardens. I like to interweave wild flowers amongst perennials in the full borders; ox eye daisy, red campion, wood anemone, betony, sweet rocket, water avens and the beautiful melancholy thistle bring an informality and freedom to the planting.

Many of these wild flowers have herbal uses. Mullein, with its thick, grey felted stems and yellow flowers, was used as a dye plant and to make candle wicks. Teasels were used in the woollen mills to raise the nap on cloth; their ripe seed heads are a magnet for goldfinches. The aromatic yarrow, which has white flowers, was used for lowering temperature and as a urinary antiseptic. Its flowers are irresistible to ladybirds and other types of beetles. Self-heal, as the name implies, was used as a herbal first aid for cuts and bruises.

Because of their wild nature, most of these native flowers will self seed readily. This again adds to the informality, with the gardener having to choose whether to let a seedling remain or take it out. Although this requires a little imagination, it adds to the fun and very often results in happy accidents and exciting combinations of plants. Marshmallow, agrimony, meadowsweet, cowslip and St. John's wort will pop up in unexpected places. Some spread out sideways like sweet violet, the grassy scented woodruff and wild strawberry.

Those Mediterranean herbs that like full sun and well-drained soil are particularly appealing to bees and butterflies. Creeping thyme gets covered in honey bees restlessly searching for nectar; butterflies love hyssop, marjoram and lavender; hover flies crowd around the purple spikes of anise hyssop. Lemon balm, traditionally planted next to hives, is much loved by bees, as is borage whose other name is bee borage. Bumble bees move greedily over chive flowers, their lazy drone helping us to relax. The air is full of movement and scent and the garden, full of herbs, is truly alive.

Hyssop

Horseradish
Armoracia rusticana

Sometimes seen growing in road verges, horseradish is a true survivor, the kind of plant still growing in long abandoned gardens along with mint and rhubarb. Its white flowers and leaves are not beautiful so it is not grown for its appearance. Coarse and waxy, they look like large dock leaves but it is what is below ground that matters: long white roots that have a hot, biting taste with a hint of sweetness. It is these that are used to make the famous horseradish sauce.

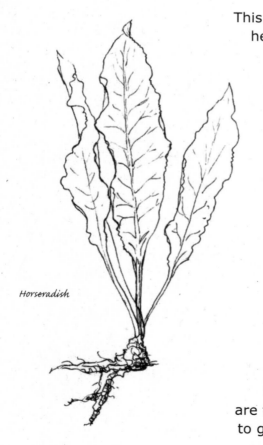

Horseradish

This is a seriously invasive herb and once you have it, it is difficult to get rid of it. If you have the space, it is best to grow it in its very own bed so that it cannot run into other plants, or in a large container. It can then be lifted, harvested and replanted which keeps its vitality and stops it getting too congested. Pot growing is one way of stopping it taking over the garden! You need to prune off finger-thick roots that are two or three years old to get the best quality for the kitchen.

Traditionally eaten with roast beef, horseradish sauce is simply made by grating the fresh root and combining it with cream or crème fraîche, mustard and a little white wine vinegar. There are other ways that this strong herb can be used and it is being rediscovered by chefs and even supermarkets where it can sometimes be bought fresh. Mustard and horseradish go together very well and make a condiment for fish, eggs or chicken or they can add extra bite to a stewed apple sauce for duck or goose. In Scandinavia, horseradish sauce is served with fried fish, where its pungency cuts through the oiliness of the frying. It has to be used in cold sauces only, as heating would damage the volatile oils that give it such zest.

Grated horseradish should be used immediately or it will darken and loose its taste. Mixing it with vinegar preserves its strong flavour but a word of warning: grating horseradish is rather like chopping onions, so have the tissues handy! An unpeeled root will keep in the fridge for a week. It is good to experiment; try adding some gratings to mayonnaise to go with seared tuna, seafood or oily fish. Alternatively, you might spice up a winter soup with a few shavings of this invigorating herb.

Horseradish
Plant type: Perennial
Height: 60cm
Ideal conditions: Good loam, but will grow almost anywhere
Uses: Culinary, medicinal

Lavender
Lavandula species and cultivars

The name lavender comes from the Latin 'lavare' which means 'to wash' and there has been a long association between this delightfully fragrant herb and washing clothes and skin. Today it is an ingredient of many soaps, bath products, skin creams, shampoos and conditioners, exactly as it has been down the centuries. In medieval days, the laundry was laid out to dry on lavender bushes to give it a fresh scent (indeed, the word 'launder' comes from the same Latin word). Sprigs of lavender were hung in clothes cupboards, made into linen sachets to deter moths or mixed with other herbs in pot pourris to scent a room.

The dried flowers can be made into a soothing herb pillow when the sedative qualities of lavender help to relieve headaches and bring sleep. This is an antiseptic herb and lavender water was used by nurses in the First World War to bathe soldiers' wounds. Lavender oil is one of the most popular aromatherapy oils, incredibly relaxing especially when mixed with geranium, a natural partnership.

Lavender

It sometimes surprises people that you can use lavender in cooking but it gives an unexpected and exciting flavour to both sweet and savoury foods. The pretty purple flowers can be sprinkled on to salads or used to decorate ice creams, sorbets or chocolate cake. Sprigs of lavender laid in sugar and left sealed for a couple of weeks give an interesting new twist to custards, puddings, baked apples and cakes. The taste of lavender becomes stronger as it is dried so you may want to experiment with using fresh and dried flowers; add them to homemade bread, biscuits and scones.

Lavender also goes with meats and is one of the ingredients of the classis *herbes de Provence.* It can even be put into a butter sauce for salmon but only small quantities should be used or the flavour can be overpowering. One of my favourite cheeses is rolled in lavender. Called Katy's White Lavender, this Yorkshire ewes' milk cheese tastes a bit like feta and its marinade of lavender flowers gives it a tangy and wonderfully unexpected taste.

There is nothing quite like the sight of acres and acres of lavender in full flower, of row upon undulating purple row covered in bees and butterflies. Although associated with Provence, there are places where you can see this in Britain: in the lavender fields of Norfolk, Hampshire or the Cotswolds or even in the Carshalton area of London, the revival of an historic lavender growing area.

Lavender
Plant type: Small shrub
Height: Varies according to variety
Ideal conditions: Full sun, well-drained soil
Uses: Culinary, medicinal, cosmetic

Lemon balm and lemon verbena
Melissa officinalis and *Aloysia triphylla*

These are two herbs that, as their names suggest, smell and taste of lemon but one is a hardy perennial and the other needs to be grown in a greenhouse. Lemon balm is an easily grown, tough perennial that was traditionally rubbed onto beehives to attract the bees to return home. Although its white flowers are very small, they are very attractive to insects; in fact the botanical name *Melissa* comes from the Greek word for a honey bee. Although rather ordinary to look at, this is an uplifting herb with a fresh stimulating scent when its leaves are squeezed.

Lemon Balm

Lemon balm produces a lot of seed and seedlings and can easily become entrenched in paths or amongst other plants so it is a good idea to cut it down right to the base just after flowering. This will in any case make it produce plenty of fresh growth for cooking. There is a lovely golden lemon balm that looks very pretty in dappled shade, brightening an area underneath shrubs and growing better out of full sun to prevent scorching. The variegated form is also good and has yellow splashed leaves.

The leaves of lemon balm can be used in cooking wherever a recipe calls for fresh lemon: as a stuffing for poultry and in salads, puddings, soups, sauces and in fish dishes. They can be steeped in fruit cups and summer punches or used to flavour and decorate ice creams. A sprig of lemon balm can be added to a pot of Earl Grey tea or made into a refreshing herb tea just on its own.

Lemon verbena makes an even better herb tea due to the intense scent of its leaves. This is a deciduous shrub that is best grown in a greenhouse or conservatory unless you live in a very fortunate part of the country. It doesn't need to have heat, but must be kept frost free. I cut it right back each autumn to its basic framework of branches and it reshoots every spring with slender pointed leaves that are full of volatile oils. These can be used in the same way as lemon balm but the taste is more perfumed and more developed. You can pack the leaves into a jar of sugar to infuse a tangy lemon flavour, which can then be used to make puddings. Both these plants can be dried for making pot pourri and for stuffing into linen sachets so their delightful lemon scents can be appreciated long after they have gone to sleep for the winter.

Lemon Verbena

Lemon Balm, Lemon Verbena
Plant type: Perennial (lemon balm), tender shrub (lemon verbena)
Height: 80cm (lemon balm), 3m unless pot grown or pruned (lemon verbena)
Ideal conditions: Sun or semi-shade (lemon balm), sun and shelter (lemon verbena)
Uses: Culinary, medicinal, pot pourri

Lovage
Levisticum officinale

Lovage is not a plant for a very small garden. Growing to 2m and with a girth of nearly the same, it does require some space but it looks magnificent at the back of a large herb border. Although it comes from the Mediterranean, it is a tough, hardy perennial that grows vigorously. Its glossy, dark green leaves are attractively divided and have a strong scent of celery mixed with a hint of yeast and angelica. The leaves grow to about 90cm whilst tall hollow stems rise above them and carry umbrella shaped heads of golden flowers followed by brown, strongly flavoured seeds.

This is a highly aromatic plant and its scent lingers on your fingers long after you have picked it. In the past lovage was grown in vegetable gardens where its stems were blanched with lightproof paper so it could be cooked like celery. Its young stems were candied like those of angelica and used for cake decoration. It even had a reputation in mediaeval days as an aphrodisiac and was used in love potions!

The commonest use for lovage nowadays is in making a springtime soup. Even the young leaves have a potent flavour so they should be used sparingly but they give a delicious, warm aromatic taste to a vegetable soup. A blend of sweated carrots and potatoes with stock and cream probably needs about two tablespoons of chopped fresh lovage but it is a matter of personal taste. Lovage creates a good stock for stews and casseroles giving a hearty quality useful for vegetarian cooking.

Tomatoes and lovage go well together, either in soups and sauces or with a little chopped leaf sprinkled on sliced beef tomatoes in a salad. A tasty herb butter can be made for melting on boiled potatoes, carrots or beans and the young leaves can even be made into fritters.

The seeds of lovage have a biting, peppery celery like flavour; sometimes when I am at work I like to slip a few green seeds into my cheese sandwiches to make them more interesting! At one time lovage seeds used to be pounded in a pestle and mortar to make a kind of pepper for seasoning meat and soups, a tradition that it might be fun to revive.

Lovage

The ripe seed may be baked in wholemeal bread or scones and with home-made cheese biscuits or oatcakes.

Lovage
Plant type: Hardy perennial
Height: Up to 2m
Ideal conditions: Rich moist soil in sun
Uses: Culinary, medicinal

Marigold
Calendula officinalis

The most brilliantly coloured flower of the herb garden is the marigold. With its vivid orange or yellow flowers it shines out on even the dullest day. This is not the African marigold (*Tagetes*) that is commonly used as a bedding plant but the old-fashioned plant that was the mainstay of many a cottage garden. Its botanical name, *Calendula*, comes from the same Latin route as the word 'calendar' because this is a flower that blooms for so many months of the year. Also known as pot marigold, this herb has been grown for many centuries for healing, cooking and beauty.

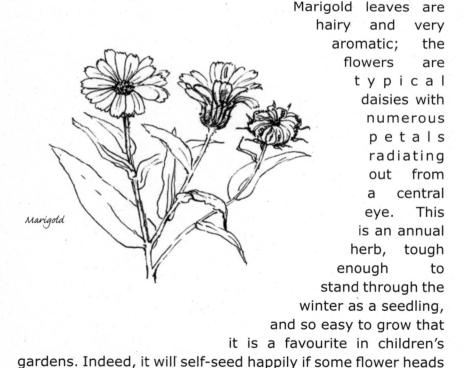

Marigold

Marigold leaves are hairy and very aromatic; the flowers are t y p i c a l daisies with numerous p e t a l s radiating out from a central eye. This is an annual herb, tough enough to stand through the winter as a seedling, and so easy to grow that it is a favourite in children's gardens. Indeed, it will self-seed happily if some flower heads are left on the plant. Regular deadheading will keep the plants bushy and produce more flowers. The original wild marigold has single flowers but there are garden cultivars with double orange, yellow, cream and apricot coloured flowers. They were bred to have double the amount of petals, not just for their visual appeal, but so that there were more petals for harvesting.

These brilliant orange petals can be strewn over salads along with other colourful herb flowers. Just pull them off the rather bitter central disk; this is a good way to get children interested in eating salads. The young leaves give a slightly peppery flavour that spices up plain lettuce. Fresh petals can also be put into cream cheese sandwiches or made into a strong infusion to be added in the early stages of cheesemaking. Marigold petals have long been used as a saffron substitute for colouring rice. Although they don't have the same intriguing favour as saffron, they do give a good yellow tint.

Calendula is one of the principal healing herbs and you can buy commercial creams for soothing sunburn, nappy rash, and treating minor wounds and skin problems. It is used in many cosmetics, face or hand creams, where it is good for skin that has been exposed to the elements. At one time marigold was used to produce a hair dye. This was commented on by William Turner, the father of English botany, in his herbal of 1551: 'Some women use to make their heyre yellow with the flowers of this herb, not being content with the natural colour which God hath given them'.

Marigold
Plant type: Hardy annual
Height: 30cm
Ideal conditions: Full sun but not very fussy
Uses: Culinary, medicinal, cosmetic, pot pourri

Marjoram
Origanum vulgare

Marjoram and oregano: these are names that create some confusion. Marjoram is a hardy perennial that has being grown for centuries in British gardens for cooking and healing. Oregano is a loose term for several different herbs (in America it may be plants that are not origanums at all) but mainly for a subspecies *Origanum vulgare subsp. hirtum,* also known as Greek oregano. It is this plant that is available commercially as dried 'oregano'. And just to be awkward, the dried herb on sale as 'marjoram' is actually the annual known as sweet or knotted marjoram, *Origanum majorana*. Both sweet marjoram and marjoram are easily grown in our gardens but oregano is best bought as a dried herb because we can never emulate the heat and poor soil that create the best flavour.

Marjoram

Flowering after the thymes, marjoram is a bee and butterfly plant par excellence, making it essential for a wildlife garden. Crowded with purple flower heads on reddish stems, it is easy to see why the ancient Greeks called it 'joy of the mountains'. There are some very colourful cultivars; golden marjorams, some with flat leaves, some crinkly; variegated marjorams with stripes of white, the best being called 'Polyphant' or gold-tipped marjoram where every leaf looks as though it has been dipped in a pot of gold paint. As well as being very ornamental in the garden, these pretty leaves look wonderful on salads or as a garnish.

The flavour of marjoram is warm like thyme but a little sweeter. That of sweet marjoram has an intense, balsamic depth that makes it a joy to use. Both these and oregano are used extensively in Italian recipes, in tomato dishes, pasta and pizza and as a topping for fresh tomatoes and mozzarella. Any of these delicious herbs can be included in vegetable and meat dishes, with rice stuffings for vegetables, in Greek salads or with egg and cheese dishes.

The way that marjoram self seeds can be a bit of a nuisance. Seedlings can get into cracks in paving or into paths so it is a good idea to cut the plant to ground level after flowering. This also makes it put on new growth suitable for cooking. In fact, it is helpful to have several plants in order to allow one to flower to attract bees and for its pretty flowers, and to cut the others down in rotation throughout the season to force fresh growth. Golden and variegated marjorams lose their attractive colouring as they flower, so this method retains their intensity.

Marjoram
Plant type: Perennial (marjoram), annual (sweet marjoram)
Height: Varied, up to 80cm
Ideal conditions: Sun, well-drained soil
Uses: Culinary, medicinal, pot pourri

Mint
Mentha species and varieties

I grow many different varieties of mint in the walled garden, each carefully planted in large black tubs so that they do not run into one another! As they start to get congested, the plants are halved and replanted so that they keep their vitality. All are topped up with fresh compost and fed every year. Having them all grown side-by-side gives visitors a chance to compare their scent, colour and texture. With so much choice, I am often asked for advice about which to use in cooking.

Spearmint is the best all-rounder. Because it has a smooth, bright green leaf it is a common favourite for classic mint sauce to go with lamb as well as for the Greek yoghurt dish *tzatziki* and Middle Eastern *tabbouleh* made with bulgur. Mint lassi is a refreshing yoghurt side dish in Indian cuisine and a good way of counteracting a fiery curry! A simple sprig of spearmint gives a good flavour to boiled potatoes or green peas but for this I also like to use applemint, which has a hairy dull green leaf. The appearance of the leaf does not matter when it is cooked with vegetables

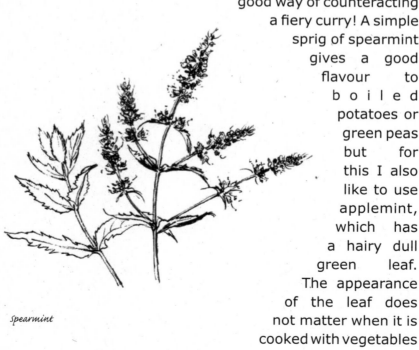

Spearmint

and it has a delicious flavour.

Peppermint has long been made into a herb tea and is very refreshing when drunk after a meal as well as aiding digestion. Its leaves have a strong scent of menthol and are used to produce peppermint oil, which is put into cooling mint creams and after dinner mints. It has wide commercial value, being an ingredient of sweets, toothpaste, chewing gum, ice cream and liqueurs. Ginger mint has a prettily striped leaf and is good in oriental cooking as well as puddings. Eau-de-Cologne mint, though a fine plant for scenting bath water or making pot pourri, is really too perfumed for cooking.

Appreciation of scent or taste is a rather personal thing, but of the many mint varieties there are plants variously described as smelling of grapefruit, apple, pineapple, lime or even chocolate. These are all useful in making puddings, especially chocolate peppermint which already smells like a sweet. Bowles mint is one of the largest of all, with grey downy leaves and long, pale, purple flower spikes. It is very attractive to insects and one summer I noticed that my huge patch of it was covered in bees. What a surprise it was though, when my son extracted honey from his hive and we found that it was strongly flavoured with mint!

There are a marvellous variety of leaf shapes and habits amongst the mints. Some have yellow stripes or cream variegation; some are purple or brilliant green, some hairy or smooth. All can be used to make pot pourri or to scent the bath water.

Spearmint
Plant type: Spreading perennial
Height: Depends on variety
Ideal conditions: Moist, rich soil in sun or part shade
Uses: Culinary, medicinal, cosmetic, confectionary, household

Parsley
Petroselinum crispum

Parsley is a herb that needs little introduction, being one of the top sellers in supermarkets and used extensively as a garnish in restaurants. It is incredibly useful for a really wide range of dishes so it makes absolute sense to grow as much as possible in the garden in order to save money and to have it to hand when needed. There are two main types: the flat leaved variety, also known as Italian or French parsley, and the decorative curled parsley. Both are hardy biennials but produce the best leaves in the first year so are perhaps best grown as an annual. There is also a variety called Hamburg parsley that has a tuberous root that is cooked like a parsnip and is popular in Europe.

Parsley

People often tell me they have difficulty with germinating parsley. This is probably because they try to sow it too early in the spring; the soil really does need to be warmed up so it is a good idea to wait until May. From then on, successive sowings can be made be in situ and those of late summer will be able to be cropped through winter and into early spring (maybe needing some protection, using a cloche). Germination can be slow so expect to wait a bit. In its second year, parsley will produce flower spikes, but cutting these out will prolong its usable harvest of leaves.

Parsley leaves are rich in vitamins and minerals as well as iron so it is a very healthy herb especially when eaten raw. The flat leaf variety has the strongest and best flavour and makes a simple and very attractive garnish. Both types are used in all sorts of ways in cooking and have been since Roman times; sprinkled over salads and tomatoes, made into herb butters, incorporated into soups, stews, sauces, stuffings and stir fries. I can't imagine cooking a fish pie or fish cakes without parsley, so important is this herb. It is an ingredient of a classic *bouquet garni* (see Bay) and a bunch will stay fresh in a jug of water for several days. If you have a surplus, it can be frozen successfully.

If parsley is chewed after eating onions or garlic it has the effect of deodorising the breath, so I always put lots of chopped leaves into garlic mayonnaise to serve with fresh crab or fried chicken. This is such a useful herb that it is worth trying to grow it even in a window box or a pot or, because it's so decorative, in a flower border. There, its rich fresh greenery makes a good edging plant to offset bright red or yellow tulips, orange cottage garden marigolds or dwarf red dahlias in autumn.

Parsley
Plant type: Biennial
Height: 25-45cm
Ideal conditions: Humus rich, moist but well-drained soil in sun
Uses: Culinary, medicinal

Rocket
Eruca sativa

Although it has been grown in England since Elizabethan times, it is only recently that there has been a surge in popularity in rocket as a culinary herb. It is now widely found in supermarkets, usually in the form of wild rocket, which has a pretty, serrated narrow leaf. An annual, it is very easy to grow; this is usually done in rows in the vegetable garden where it is sown in situ. There are various different types of seeds available that give a variety of leaf shapes; some are closer to the wild rocket, some are the traditional cultivated form.

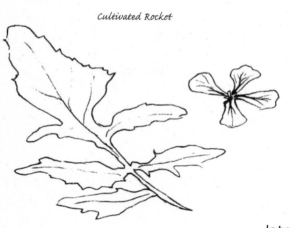

Cultivated Rocket

Cultivated rocket has tongue-shaped leaves that have a curious hot, nutty taste. The flowers are creamy white, the four petals being spaced apart to look like the sails of windmills. Both leaves and flowers are delicious in salads and, when planted in late summer, can even be harvested in winter.

Being a member of the mustard family, rocket has a rather bitter, cress-like flavour with bite to it and, being rich in vitamin C and iron, makes a healthy addition to a salad. It has been cooked as a vegetable in the Mediterranean since Roman days and is still very much an ingredient in Italian recipes. Popular on pizzas, rocket is added at the very end of cooking so that the leaves just wilt. It is also pounded and made into a pesto that is delicious on pasta dishes. Delia describes this herb as being one of her favourites and having a 'concentrated buttery flavour'.

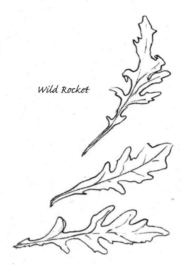

Wild Rocket

Wild rocket is the type most often seen in supermarkets and has a narrower, lobed leaf and a stronger flavour concentrated into a smaller leaf area than the cultivated plant. Its flavour is hot and spicy and it is variously known as 'roquette' (the French name) or 'rucola' (the Italian one). You can also buy seeds of this form and eat its leaves, flowers and sprouted seeds.

Wild Rocket

In the Mediterranean it is put into a rustic salad known as 'wild greens' or, when plentiful, cooked like spinach. In Provence, rocket is an important ingredient of a winter salad of baby leaves, which is known as 'mesclun'. This is a quick and easy herb to grow, perfectly happy in containers, and suitable for even the smallest garden.

Rocket
Plant type: Annual
Height: 50cm
Ideal conditions: Sun, fertile soil
Uses: Culinary, medicinal

Rosemary
Rosmarinus officinalis

The name Rosemary comes from the Latin 'dew of the sea' for this is a coastal Mediterranean herb growing on dry, scrubby hillsides and filling the air with its resinous scent. Harvested from the wild, it gave a distinctive flavour to Italian and southern French cooking, where its strong flavour could mix with the equally strong flavours of garlic, onions, red wine and meat.

There are thousands of years of folklore and custom woven into the history of this wonderful herb; scenting the Romans' bathwater, believed to safeguard against evil, burnt as a purifying herb in sick chambers, it was also carried at weddings and funerals. Shakespeare referred to its link with memory; as Hamlet's Ophelia says, 'There's rosemary, that's for remembrance; pray, love, remember'.

Rosemary

If I had to choose a favourite herb, this would be it. The smell of rosemary fills the kitchen when it is liberally sprinkled on roasting potatoes or the Italian bread focaccia. I find it irresistible in the garden and have to squeeze its camphorous leaves on passing. For this reason it was often planted on either side of a mediaeval doorway, with sprigs of rosemary being strewn on the floor or burnt over hot embers to scent the room. It was used in the still room, where all the beauty preparations of the house were made, for hair rinses, toilet waters, pot pourri and linen sachets. Still widely used in commercial cosmetics, it is found in shampoos, soaps and skin creams.

Fresh rosemary is best; the dried herb can be sharp and pierce the gums. Its robust flavour goes excellently with roast lamb, the sprig being removed before serving, or cooks well with roasted vegetables or in aubergine dishes. Rosemary makes delicious cheese biscuits, but it's equally good in sweets, for flavouring honey and sugar. The pale blue flowers can be sprinkled on salads or used to decorate puddings and ice creams. In summer, rosemary can be burnt on the barbecue to give a wonderful smoky flavour to meat and fish.

There are many different types of rosemary to grow, some with pink, white or rich blue flowers, some like the rather less hardy prostrate rosemary drooping over walls or making an upright shrub like 'Miss Jessopp's'. Generally though, rosemary tends to sprawl and become lopsided but this is a natural habit. Remembering its origins, it needs full sun and an easily drained soil; what it really dislikes is a combination of winter wet and cold. Constant harvesting acts as pruning and keeps bushes more compact.

Rosemary
Plant type: Shrub
Height: 1.5m
Ideal conditions: Full sun, well-drained soil, shelter
Uses: Culinary, medicinal, cosmetic

Sage
Salvia officinalis

There are hundreds of different types of sage or *Salvia* worldwide and most are highly aromatic. Apart from the common sage used in cooking, I grow pineapple sage for its brilliant red flowers, blackcurrant sage which has fruity leaves, clary sage which has sticky mauve flowers and the gloriously named Jupiter's distaff (*Salvia glutinosa*) with resinous yellow flowers. Common sage has several very pretty coloured forms, which make excellent garden plants as well as being used for decorating food. Purple sage, golden sage and tricolour sage are shrubs that look wonderful in a flower border or spilling over the edge of a path. Ordinary sage itself has greyish felted leaves and spires of purple blue flowers that are very attractive to bees.

Very often sage becomes a leggy, straggly bush so it is important to keep it pruned and compact. Regular harvesting for the kitchen helps to do this but an additional pruning in spring makes for a better shrub. As you may lose it if you cut hard into the old wood, it is important to do this from its first or second year so that each year it can be cut back quite low down. The less common broad leaved sage hardly ever flowers so all its vitality goes into leaf formation; this makes it a good culinary plant and also less likely to become gangly. It makes a large domed shrub that can be pruned quite hard. The non-flowering variety 'Berggarten' is particularly good with wide, rounded felted leaves.

Sage has a strong flavour and can match equally strongly flavoured foods. It gives the attractive marbling to Sage Derby cheese and can be cooked with fatty meats, such as goose, duck and pork. Of course, it is used for traditional poultry stuffing. Some cookery books will advise caution in using sage but sometimes its robust taste can be quite wonderful as in the Tuscan sauce *Burro e salvia* made of butter and lots of sage leaves. It also gives a delicious pungent flavour to pan-cooked chicken rolled in parma ham in a crème fraîche sauce.

sage

This is an antiseptic herb, an infusion of which makes a good gargle for sore throats or a cleansing mouth wash. A leaf rubbed over teeth will clean them and help combat gum infections as well.

An evergreen shrub, sage can be harvested for much of the year, but to store sage for winter it can either be frozen or easily air dried.

Sage
Plant type: Shrub
Height: Up to 60cm
Ideal conditions: Full sun, well-drained soil
Uses: Culinary, medicinal
Comment: Should be avoided by epileptics and not used in medicinal quantities during pregnancy

Savory
Satureja montana and *Satureja hortensis*

These are two highly aromatic herbs, one a perennial and one an annual, which are both rich in volatile oils. Winter savory makes a small evergreen bush that looks rather like a thyme at first glance. It blooms late in the season bearing small white or palest lilac flowers and has narrow spiky leaves. Bees are attracted to it and it is a useful source of early autumn nectar. Summer savory has a rather different habit, being more upright, but has very similar flowers. As it matures, or if it gets very dry, its leaves start to turn a pretty rusty purple. Being an annual, it is often grown in rows in the vegetable garden, alongside basil, parsley or coriander. The botanical name probably comes from the Greek *satyrus* for a satyr, the woodland attendant of Dionysus, and alludes to their alleged aphrodisiac qualities!

Savory

Both winter and summer savory are known as 'bean herbs' due to their anti-flatulent properties! (Perhaps that's why they are supposed to put one in the mood for love...) They aid the digestion of pulses and fresh beans or peas as well as fatty foods.

The flavour of summer savory is somewhat sweeter and more redolent of thyme than is winter savory, which has a rather harsher taste. Both are strong and need to be added carefully but will stand lengthy cooking. They are much used in France where their slightly bitter flavour is valued for cutting through oily meats and casseroles. A soft Provencale cheese is made from unpasteurised sheep's milk flavoured with wild savory known as 'Poivre d'ane' (literally 'donkey pepper').

These rather less common herbs can be substituted for thyme or oregano in a variety of recipes, especially strongly flavoured Mediterranean dishes: in stuffed tomatoes, aubergines or peppers, making a herb crust for chicken fillets, or in a herbed terrine of pork bound in pancetta. A good herb butter can be made from the leaves of either type of savory. Chop them up very finely and blend them with softened butter to spread on savoury biscuits, blinis or thin slices of ciabatta; put a dollop on steamed broad beans or carrots or use to top jacket potatoes.

Winter savory does well in a poor well-drained soil and regular clipping helps to keep it compact. It can be used as a low hedge in an ornamental herb garden in the same way as wall germander or rock hyssop. It was grown and loved in the Elizabethan era and was sometimes used to form the shapes of knot gardens. For today's small gardens, savory is a neat aromatic herb that needs to be more widely grown.

Savory
Plant type: Perennial (winter savory), annual (summer savory)
Height: 35cm
Ideal conditions: Full sun, well drained soil
Uses: Culinary, medicinal

Sorrel
Rumex acetosa and Rumex scutatus

Making a soup with fresh young sorrel leaves is one of the joys of spring. They have a pleasant, sharp lemony taste and combined with potato, onion and stock can be blended to a bright green purée, emblematic of the season. There are two types of sorrel, both of which make a good soup: common sorrel which looks a bit like a dock and the more refined, French sorrel which has smaller shield-shaped leaves. Both are very easy to cultivate and can be sown from seed or multiplied by division. After a few years the plants should be split and replanted, or the flavour will deteriorate. Common sorrel sends up a tall flower spike that is a mass of reddish brown; this takes vitality away from the plant and is best cut out. There is a rare non-flowering form that retains all its energy for making leaves.

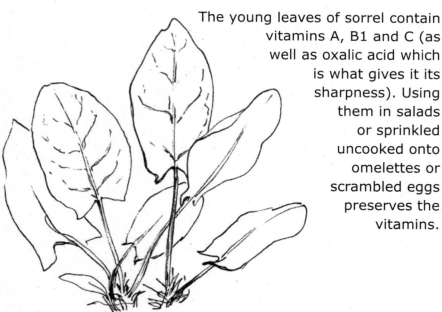

The young leaves of sorrel contain vitamins A, B1 and C (as well as oxalic acid which is what gives it its sharpness). Using them in salads or sprinkled uncooked onto omelettes or scrambled eggs preserves the vitamins.

sorrel

It is this lemon acidity that makes sorrel such a good partner for oily fish such as mackerel, trout or salmon or for rich meat such as duck or goose. A delicious sorrel sauce can be made for serving with fish, known as green sauce; the herb is mashed with a little vinegar and sugar to give piquancy for cutting through the oiliness. Wrapping meat in sorrel leaves has the effect of tenderising it.

Sorrel combines very well with spinach, that equally tangy vegetable, but if you dislike the sharp taste of the oxalic acid, boiling in two changes of water will cut down on the bitterness. As summer progresses, so does the acidity, so sorrel is best eaten in spring. This is also the best time of year for the highly decorative herb, bloody sorrel, which has pointed leaves deeply veined in red and purple. A stunning looking plant, it is particularly beautiful when backlit by the sun and I use it in the flower borders where it is combined with low pink flowered hardy geraniums and the silvery felted leaves of lychnis. Bloody sorrel is happy growing beside ponds but is versatile and makes an unusual and interesting plant for a container. Its young, tender leaves add colour and texture to salads.

Sorrel
Plant type: Perennial
Height: 70cm (common sorrel), 25cm (French sorrel)
Ideal conditions: Versatile
Uses: Culinary, dye plant
Comments: Should not be eaten by people who must avoid oxalic acid, for example people with a tendency to kidney stones

Tarragon
Artemisia dracunculus

There are two types of tarragon, French and Russian, and it is important to learn the difference: the first has a delicious flavour but is not entirely hardy, the second may be hardy but it is coarse and has very little taste. As French tarragon can only be grown from cuttings, not seed, it is sometimes sold as 'tarragon' by garden centres because it is easier to produce! You really do need to get the real thing. This has a wonderful rich anise flavour and you can tell it is the French variety by the way the smooth, undivided leaf bruises easily. I grow mine in the soil of an unheated greenhouse but in warmer parts of the country it may be possible to grow it outside in a sheltered spot.

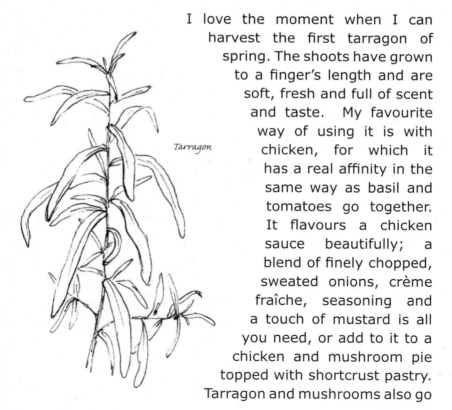

Tarragon

I love the moment when I can harvest the first tarragon of spring. The shoots have grown to a finger's length and are soft, fresh and full of scent and taste. My favourite way of using it is with chicken, for which it has a real affinity in the same way as basil and tomatoes go together. It flavours a chicken sauce beautifully; a blend of finely chopped, sweated onions, crème fraîche, seasoning and a touch of mustard is all you need, or add to it to a chicken and mushroom pie topped with shortcrust pastry. Tarragon and mushrooms also go well together and it is used to flavour commercial vegetarian pâtés.

Tarragon is penetrating enough to be cooked with salmon, which has a strong flavour of its own, and it can be used in small quantities with other fish too. It is good with eggs, enhancing a cheese and mushroom omelette in particular, and is one of the ingredients of the classic *fines herbes*. Tarragon can be steeped in white wine vinegar for adding, when mature, to salad dressings and sauces; a sprig of the herb looks very attractive in the bottle and makes a good home made present. Another way of preserving its flavour is by freezing which it does successfully but don't bother trying to dry it as it won't keep its subtlety.

Although you can't grow French tarragon from seed, it is easy to create more plants from its roots. If you take a sharp knife, you can detach a rooted piece from the parent plant and simply re-pot that. The name tarragon comes from the French *esdragon*, also known as *Herbe au Dragon,* and alludes to its ancient reputation for curing snake bite. I am very fond of the 'little dragon' in my greenhouse.

Tarragon
Plant type: Perennial
Height: 75-90cm
Ideal conditions: Shelter, sun, frost protection & well drained soil
Uses: Culinary

Thyme
Thymus species and cultivars

There are so many different types of thyme, all wonderful aromatic garden plants, for planting at the front of flower borders, on a rock garden or in tubs and window boxes. The National Collection of Thyme is held in Chesters Walled Garden, and when I take visitors around I am often asked if you can eat them all. All are technically edible but you may not want to flavour your food with some of the more unusual properties such as pine resin or camphor! There is a whole gamut of scents ranging from orange and lemon through culinary thyme to caraway and eucalyptus.

Thyme

The plants vary visually as well with amazing diversity of flower and leaf colour, height and spread. The traditional thyme used for cooking is *Thymus vulgaris*, a small sprawling, evergreen bush with pale mauve flowers. Its leaves are grey green and narrow and plants from garden centres are very variable depending on whether they are grown from seed or cuttings. A native of the Mediterranean, thyme needs a well drained, slightly alkaline soil and full sun, imitating as nearly as possible the rocky hillsides of Provence or Spain, where it scents the warm air. It gives a characteristic flavour to the cooking of this area, being one of the eight herbs of *herbes de Provence* and included in the classic *bouquet garni.*

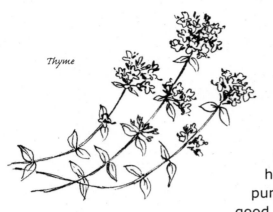

Thyme

Thyme has a strong flavour so it goes well with red meat and game or richly flavoured casseroles, slowly cooked with garlic, onions and red wine. It can be used fresh or dried, the latter having a stronger, more pungent flavour. Thyme is good in stuffings for poultry or as part of a herb crust for meat or fish, as well as for baked vegetables or roasted garlic dishes. Used carefully, the fresh herb gives a warm flavour to winter soups such as cream of leek and potato. Lemon thyme has a rather more delicate flavour so it cooks well with less robust meats such as chicken or with fish, stuffings and soups. Leaves of lemon or orange thyme, together with their flowers, can be scattered on summer salads.

Regular harvesting of thyme sprigs will help to keep a bush compact, but it should still be clipped over lightly after flowering. Start doing this from its second year but do not cut into the old wood. Even the mat-forming creeping thymes benefit from having their ends clipped back. Many of these carpeting plants are cultivars of wild British thymes but they still need plenty of sand and grit worked into the soil, as they grow naturally in rocky upland areas, like the switchback curves of Hadrian's Wall. Grow them between paving slabs or by a bench to give a delightful scent every time you walk on them.

Thyme
Plant type: Small, evergreen shrub or mat-forming carpeter
Height: Up to 40cm depending on variety
Ideal conditions: Full, well-drained soil
Uses: Culinary, medicinal

Common and Botanical Names
Mentioned in this Book

Common Name	Botanical Name
Agrimony	*Agrimonia eupatoria*
Angelica, purple leaved	*Angelica gigas*
Anise hyssop	*Agastache foeniculum*
Basil	*Ocimum basilicum*
Basil, Greek or bush	*Ocimum minimum*
Basil, holy	*Ocimum sanctum*
Bay	*Laurus nobilis*
Bay, golden	*Laurus nobilis* 'Aurea'
Bay, narrow leaved	*Laurus nobilis* f.*angustifolia*
Borage	*Borago officinalis*
Borage, perennial	*Borago laxiflora*
Chamomile	*Chamaemelum nobile*
Chamomile, non-flowering	*Chamaemelum nobile* 'Treneague'
Chervil	*Anthriscus cerefolium*
Chives	*Allium schoenoprasum*
Coriander	*Coriandrum sativum*
Cowslip	*Primula veris*
Dill	*Anethum graveolens*
Evening primrose	*Oenethera biennis*
Fennel	*Foeniculum vulgare*
Fennel, bronze	*Foeniculum vulgare* 'Atropurpureum'
Fennel, Florence	*Foeniculum vulgare* var. 'Dulce'
Garlic	*Allium sativum*
Garlic, wild	*Allium ursinum*
Horseradish	*Armoracia rusticana*
Hyssop	*Hyssopus aristatus*
Lavender	*Lavandula* sp.
Lemon balm	*Melissa officinalis*
Lemon verbena	*Aloysa triphylla*
Lovage	*Levisticum officinale*
Marigold	*Calendula officinalis*
Marjoram	*Origanum vulgare*
Marjoram, sweet	*Origanum majorana*

Marshmallow	*Althea officinalis*
Meadowsweet	*Filipendula ulmaria*
Mint, apple	*Mentha suaveolens*
Mint, Bowles	*Mentha x villosa* var. *alepecuroides*
Mint, chocolate	*Mentha x piperita f.citrata* 'Chocolate'
Mint, Eau-de-Cologne	*Mentha x piperita f.citrata*
Mint, grapefruit	*Mentha x piperita f.citrata* 'Grapefruit'
Mint, lime	*Mentha x piperita f.citrata* 'Lime'
Mint, Moroccan	*Mentha spicata* var.*crispa* 'Moroccan'
Mint, pepper	*Mentha x piperita*
Mint, pineapple	*Mentha suaveolens* 'Variegata'
Mint, spear	*Mentha spicata*
Mullein	*Verbascum thapsus*
Nasturtium	*Tropaeolum majus*
Oregano	*Origanum vulgare* subsp. *hirtum*
Parsley	*Petroselinum crispum*
Parsley, French	*Petroselinum c.* var. *neopolitanum*
Parsley, Hamburg	*Petroselinum c.* var. *tuberosum*
Rocket	*Eruca sativa*
Rosemary	*Rosmarinus officinalis*
Savory, summer	*Satureja montana*
Savory, winter	*Satureja hortensis*
Self-heal	*Prunella vulgaris*
Sorrel	*Rumex acetosa*
Sorrel, bloody	*Rumex sanguineus*
Sorrel, French	*Rumex scutatus*
St. John's wort	*Hypericum perforatum*
Sweet cicely	*Myrrhis odorata*
Tarragon, French	*Artemisia dracunculus*
Tarragon, Russian	*Artemisia* subsp. *dracunculoides*
Thyme	*Thymus* sp.
Violet	*Viola odorata*
Wild strawberry	*Fragraria vesca*
Woodruff	*Galium odoratum*
Yarrow	*Achillea millefolium*

Suggested further reading

Some of these books may be out of print, but they can probably be obtained via a book search website.

A Modern Herbal – Mrs M Grieve (Tiger) Published in 1931 and out of date in some areas, especially medicinally, but a classic and full of fascinating information
Sophie Grigson's Herbs – Sophie Grigson (BBC Books) for excellent recipes
Oriental Vegetables – Joy Larkcom (John Murray)
Herb Society's Complete Medicinal Herbal – Penelope Ody (Dealerfield)
RHS Encyclopaedia of Herbs – Deni Bown (Dorling Kindersley)
Herb Garden Design – Ethne Clarke (Frances Lincoln)
Chinese Herbal Medicine – Daniel P Reid (Thorsons)
Herbs – Roger Phillips and Nicky Foy (Pan)
Herb Gardens and Tea 2006/7 Barty Phillips (Margaretta Publishing) – for places to visit (with a cup of tea nearby!)
Food for Free – Richard Mabey (Collins)
Herbal: The Essential Guide to Herbs for Living – Deni Bown (Chelsea Physic Garden)
Gardens of Northumberland and the Borders – Susie White (Sanderson Books)
The Yellow Book – the National Gardens Scheme, published annually for ideas of herb gardens to visit

Internet

Mrs Grieve's Modern Herbal on line – www.botanical.com
Delia Smith's website with recipes and ingredients lists - www.deliaonline.com
The Herb Society – www.herbsociety.co.uk
The National Herb Centre – www.herbcentre.co.uk